Daniel
the Warrior

Written by Monét Lynne Clark

Illustrated by Sarah K. Turner

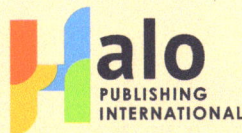

Halo
PUBLISHING
INTERNATIONAL

ISBN: 978-1-61244-856-5
Library of Congress Control Number: 2020909200

Printed in the United States of America

Halo Publishing International
8000 W Interstate 10
Suite 600
San Antonio, Texas 78230
www.halopublishing.com
contact@halopublishing.com

To my son Demetris "Deme."

You will always be Mommy's WARRIOR!

"Daniel, it's time to wake up," Mommy says.

Today is my first day at a new school. My new school is sooo big. Quick! I need to hide so Mommy can't make me go to school.

This is a good place. Mommy won't find me here.

"DANIEL!" Mommy walks right in and finds me under the bed. "Daniel, what are you doing? You're going to be late for your first day."

"Mommy, what if I get lost and can't find my classroom? Please let me stay home."

See? Even Roxy wants me to stay home.

"What if the kids laugh at the way I talk?"

"Daniel, you don't have to be scared. You're special,"
Mommy tells me and gives me a kiss on the cheek.
"You are a warrior! You got this!"

I get dressed, put on my favorite blue shoes, and get into the car.

"Daniel, don't forget you have your helmet and shield." Mommy says I have a helmet and shield because I am a warrior. "Give me a hug, Daniel. You got this!"

"I am a warrior. I am a warrior," I say to myself, climbing the steps of the big school.

I make it to my classroom all by myself!

My teacher, Mrs. Patterson, makes all of us say our names.

I don't like talking in front of people. When I am scared, it is hard for me to talk and I stutter. Maybe I should ask Mrs. Patterson to send me to the nurse. Maybe she will skip over me.

Please skip me. Please skip me.

"Next," Mrs. Patterson says, pointing at me. Everyone looks at me.

"My name is D-D-D-Daniel."

Some of the kids start laughing. Mrs. Patterson makes them stop, but I still feel sad.

Finally, it's my favorite part of the day: RECESS!

"Hi Daniel, d-d-do-o-o you want to-o-o play?"
asks Xavier.

Wow, Xavier talks like me. Off we go to the swings.

We hear some other kids saying, "Look at the babies!
Baby talk, baby talk."

Recess ends and Mrs. Patterson tells us all to line up
and go inside to the classroom.

It is my second day of school. I can't wait to see Xavier.

At lunch, I ask Xavier, "Do you want to be a warrior?"

"What's a warrior?" Xavier asks me.

"My mommy said a warrior is brave. If we close our eyes, a helmet and shield show up.

"YES! I want to be a warrior, too!" Xavier shouts.

"We need a word to use when we close our eyes," I say.

"How about *SAWDATACIOUS!*" Xavier yells.

"Yes! *SAWDATACIOUS!*"

SAWDATACIOUS!

Back at recess, we hear from the same boys as yesterday.

"Daniel and Xavier, baby talk, baby talk."

Xavier and I close our eyes and scream, "*SAWDATACIOUS!*
SAWDATACIOUS!"

BAM! Our helmets and shields appear! And I can't hear anything the boys are saying.

Xavier and I start to laugh. Mommy was right! I am a WARRIOR! My helmet and shield work!

And, you know what? It's okay that I talk a little different because I *am* different. I am a WARRIOR!

After dinner, Mommy asks, "Daniel, how was your day?"

"It was GREAT! I don't want to miss tomorrow."

Mommy laughs and kisses me goodnight. "Daniel, I love you."

This new school isn't so bad after all.

Questions:

1. Why was Daniel afraid on his first day of school?

2. How did Daniel feel when the kids teased him?

3. Have you ever felt afraid at school? Why?

4. How can you be a warrior if someone is teasing you or a friend?

5. Who are two people you can go to for help if you are being teased?